# Powerful Presentations

Dawn Frail

ISBN:  1-897212-00-3
ISBN-13:  978-1-897212-00-4

"To dream anything that you want to dream. That is the beauty of the human mind. To do anything that you want to do. That is the strength of the human will. To trust yourself to test your limits. That is the courage to succeed."

~ Bernard Edmonds

# CONTENTS

# 1 INTRODUCTION

In many situations in our lives, we are called upon to make presentations. When we are at work presenting the latest project, we all do our best to muster up the courage and pull together the skills we likely haven't used since college or university. Or so we think.

What we fail to realize is that asking for a raise is a presentation. Expressing an opinion to the PTA is a presentation. So is talking to the City Council or the Sunday morning congregation. Whether at work, at home, or in the community, we all are making presentations, or speeches, all the time. We can be more effective in any of these areas by using some simple and basic techniques to organize our thoughts and our delivery.

One place we see the biggest impact in making professional and powerful presentations is, of course, at work. The rewards for being a confident and competent speaker are many. One way to gain visibility in your company is to deliver impressive presentations. You can make a good impression on supervisor and subordinate alike by being a skilled communicator. You can earn a position on a desirable high-profile project by demonstrating your ability to speak. You can even put yourself in a better position for the next promotion. And in hard times, when it comes down to who to keep and who to let go, you will be more of an asset to the company if you give examples of you superior communication ability.

So when it comes to your career, if you want to be successful, becoming a powerful presenter can be a huge stepping stone to getting you there. Even when it comes to every day life, getting your opinions and ideas heard is a satisfying experience.

The power of being a great communicator has the power to make you great. Apply the techniques, apply yourself, and reap the rewards.

## 2 HANDLING NERVOUSNESS

"There is no such thing as bravery;
only degrees of fear."

~ John Wainwright

## PRACTICE, PRACTICE, PRACTICE

Practice is, by far, the most effective way to reduce nervousness. It works for every person, every presentation, every time. No matter what else you do, this is the one thing that brings dramatic results.

Be sure to practice effectively by following these guidelines:

1. Begin practicing as soon as possible, and pace yourself. Don't wait until the last minute. You can't cram for a speech like it's a college exam. Instead, practice two or three times per day for two or three weeks.
2. Practice out loud. Speeches often 'sound' different than they 'read.'
3. Get an audience. Your spouse, your kids, your cat – anyone will do.
4. Practice in front of the mirror. This seems to be the most popular technique.
5. Tape record your speech. Then listen to it objectively.
6. Practice at the actual location. This isn't always possible, but if it is, take advantage.

## TAKE A DEEP BREATH

When faced with a stressful situation, our bodies instinctively take over. Often our breathing becomes very shallow and our lungs don't fully inflate with fresh air. As a result, toxins accumulate.

In order to get the bad air (toxins) out, we need to put the good air (fresh oxygen) in. Take a few very deep breaths, then remain aware of your breathing pattern. In particular, do this while you're being introduced. It simply makes you feel better.

An added benefit to having nice, full lungs is that you will have the air you need to let your voice carry clearly. You will also have plenty of strength left in your voice to ensure your sentences don't trail off.

## STICK TO SUBJECTS YOU ARE PASSIONATE ABOUT

If there is a gold rule when it comes to giving speeches, this is it.

A dull, emotionless presentation is as much a bore for the audience as it is a failure for the speaker.

Passion can help you overcome nervousness for two reasons.

First, when you're passionate about your subject, you're probably also very knowledgeable. As a result, your confidence will soar.

Second, when you speak with passion, your emotion and excitement flow naturally. It's very easy to forget about your nervousness once you get caught up in your own excitement.

## USE PERSONAL STORIES

Very often nervousness stems from the fear of appearing foolish if and when we forget what we want to say. We're afraid of going blank.

One way to handle this particular fear is to use personal stories and real-life experiences in your presentation.

We rarely forget the details of a personal experience. Because we were there, we know what happened, and we know what came next. It's the one part of your presentation where you don't need to worry about forgetting the details. The more of these you have, the less room for fear and nervousness.

## MEMORIZE YOUR INTRODUCTION

For anyone who experiences nervousness when speaking, the time you feel most nervous is, without a doubt, the first two minutes. Once you get past this point, the rest of the presentation usually flows smoothly. But first you have to get through the first two minutes.

By memorizing your introduction, you'll be able to fly on 'autopilot' right through the worst part. Introductions are often short and therefore not difficult to memorize. Once you get past this point, you'll find you have probably calmed down considerably, and you will ultimately cruise through the remainder of the presentation.

# 3 CONTENT

"Let thy speech be short, comprehending much in few words."

~ Apocrypha, Ecclesiasticus

## HAVE A CLEAR PURPOSE

There are four main purposes:

- Inform.
    - o   To give your audience information (i.e., a briefing)

- Entertain.
    - o   To provide enjoyment for your audience (i.e., a roast)

- Persuade.
    - o   To convince your audience of something (i.e., a campaign speech)

- Motivate.
    - o   To give a call to action (i.e., a fundraiser)

Whatever your purpose, know what it is before you begin to prepare your presentation. Write it down and keep it in front of you. As you develop your speech, develop your points and examples to match your purpose. If they're weak or don't fit, don't use them.

If you stick to one main purpose, your audience will easily understand your point, and you'll be a smashing success.

## KEEP IT SHORT

The more you say, the less people remember. No presentation should be longer than necessary. If you have your purpose clearly painted in your mind, staying on track is easier.

As a general rule, keep it to a maximum of three points. In an extremely long presentation you may be able to get away with more, but in most cases stick to three or less. In a short presentation, limit yourself to one main point.

Limiting yourself may seem difficult at first since you will invariably have more to say. But unfortunately far too many presenters fall into the trap of saying too much.

Also, avoid the temptation to add sub-points to your main points. That is one way to sneak in more information, but once your audience begins to have difficulty following you, you risk losing them altogether.

Do yourself and your audience a favour – keep it short.

## GET THEIR ATTENTION WITH THE FIRST SENTENCE

You have only one chance to make a good first impression, and according to the latest set of experts you have about three seconds to make it. You may think that in three seconds you barely have time to smile and say, "Hello," let alone make an impression.

However, your first sentence has to grab their attention and make them want to hear more. You should also make use of vocal variety and visual impact.

Popular ways to begin a presentation are to:

- Ask a question
- Give an appropriate quote
- Give a startling fact or statistic
- Demonstrate something
- Tell a personal story
- Give an anecdote
- Say or do something humourous
- Show a unique prop

Any of these methods should be successful in starting you off on the right foot.

## CUE YOUR CONCLUSION

There are two points in your presentation when you can be certain you have your audience's attention – after you have been introduced, and after you say, "in conclusion."

People don't always tune out or fade away purposely, but they *always* pay attention when they know the end is coming. Most conclusions (all good ones) contain a summary of the speaker's main points.  So, if in fact members of your audience have been caught snoozing, they know they can still get the gist of the presentation at the end.

Simply saying, "in conclusion" will do the trick, but it's a little boring. Try a nice, long pause instead.  A summarizing statement or question ("So, what have learned this hour?"), will also do nicely, as will turning up the house lights or coming way out in front of the lectern.

## TELL TEM, TELL THEM, TELL THEM

When it comes to speech organization there is one simple rule you should follow without fail:

*Tell them what you're going to tell them.*
*Tell them.*
*Tell them what you told them.*

It may seem a bit repetitious at first glance, but when used properly, it is a very powerful technique.

In your introduction let your listeners know what's coming – tell them what you're going to tell them.  Your statement of purpose will help you here.  If you fail to tell them what's coming, they'll try to figure it out on their own instead of giving you their full attention.

In the body of your speech, give them the information you want them to know – tell them.

Finally, in your conclusion, summarize your main points – tell them what you told them.

Once you experience how powerful this technique is, you will use it every time.

# 4 DELIVERY

"We are not won by arguments that we can analyze but by tone and temper, by the manner which is man himself."

~ Samuel Butler

## SMILE

Remembering to smile throughout your presentation is very important. Even as you walk to the front of the room after your introduction, all eyes are on you, judging you. You can begin to make a good first impression if you have a nice, big smile. Then keep smiling throughout your presentation, even as you go back to your seat after your conclusion. The more you smile, the more professional you appear.

Smiling during your presentation is more important than many people realize. If you present your information with a frown or solemn face, you are more likely to encounter criticism or opposition. Unfortunately, however, smiling and talking is easier said than done for many people. It is something that requires practice, but the payoff is certainly worth the effort. Even when your subject is of a serious nature, a small smile can make the world of difference.

## PAUSE BEFORE YOU BEGIN

If you want to be a powerful presenter, make a powerful impression immediately by doing something very simple.

When you're standing confidently at the front of the room, wait for the applause to die down, smile and give a nice, long pause while looking out over the audience.

A common mistake people make is to begin speaking right away, before the audience finishes clapping, and sometimes even before they finish shaking the hand of their introducer. By doing that, they have robbed themselves of a very powerful moment.

Sometimes it can be difficult to simply stand there composed and confidently silent as a room full of people stare expectantly up at you. But if you can muster up the control, you can have your audience in the palm of your hand.

## MAKE EYE CONTACT WITH AS MANY PEOPLE AS POSSIBLE

People enjoy a presentation and feel good about the speaker when they have 'connected.' This is that all-important rapport that must be built between speaker and listener. One of the best ways to accomplish this is by the use of eye contact. The more people with whom you can make eye contact, the more people will feel connected.

The most important aspect of eye contact is to hold it long enough for the audience to feel the contact. Eye contact seems much longer to the speaker than it does to the audience, so it is important to hold eye contact with each person longer than seems necessary. About three to five seconds is a good average, which is about the length of a short sentence.

Another way to make eye contact powerful is to combine it with a genuine smile. If you get a smile in return, or a knowing nod, you'll know you've been successful in making contact and building rapport.

## GET OUT FROM BEHIND THE LECTERN

The more your audience can see of you, the more they like it.

There are certain situations, however, when it is difficult – or even impossible – to get away from the lectern. If, for example, your audience is very large and the microphone is fixed to the lectern, you must remain in that spot. But even in that situation you may be able to stretch the microphone over to one side and stand beside the lectern.

In all other situations, you should get out front if you want to make a powerful impression. When unencumbered by the stand, you can show off your confidence, you can make effective use of powerful gestures, and you can get physically closer to your audience. All of those techniques make you a more powerful presenter.

## MAKE YOUR LAST STATEMENT A POWERFUL ONE

The last impression you leave is just as important as the first impression you make. Your conclusion has to be effective in summarizing your main points and it must include your call to action. In order for you to leave a powerful impression, the last thing you say must be loud, forceful, and commanding. Occasionally people will end on a soft note, often with a questioning tone. Although this may seem like the natural thing to do, you rob yourself of a powerful opportunity.

Choose your last sentence carefully. Make certain it says what you want people to remember – and then be sure to practice it over and over and over (in an attempt to be loud and forceful, we can end up yelling at our audience). Ending a speech this way is not always natural, so practice until the inflection and emphasis reflect the best way to make the powerful impression you want to make.

# 5 VISUAL AIDS

"A picture is worth more than
a thousand words."

~ Chinese Proverb

## USE VISUAL AIDS TO ENHANCE

A common mistake often occurs when using visual aids. The aid – be it a flipchart, slides, video, etc. – tends to become the main attraction. In fact, without the aid, one wonders if there would be any presentation at all.

This is the result of building your speech around your visual aids, instead of using them properly to emphasize your point. To prevent this from happening to you, develop your presentation first, *then* choose the best visual aid to emphasize the point that needs it.

Visual aids should be used for clarification emphasis, and in some cases, for interest. But they should be kept to a minimum to ensure they don't dominate.

## HIT AS MANY SENSES AS POSSIBLE

The more senses we touch with our visual aids, the more our audience retains. Sometimes our audience is too large to utilize all the senses, but if we are able, we should use more than just one or two.

Hearing is not only used to listen to the meaning of your words, but also to hear an infinite number of available sound effects. Sight is very effective since we know a picture is 'worth more than a thousand words.' Demonstration is a powerful technique.

Using touch requires a little more imagination if you have a large audience. You must utilize something everyone already has access to – their skin, hair, or clothes, for example. Of course with a small audience, you can have loads of fun with this one.

Taste and smell are other challenges if your audience is large, but don't give up on them too soon. The more senses you can put into action, the more information they'll retain – and for a longer period of time.

## DON'T KEEP PROPS IN FRONT OF YOU

When it comes to visual aids, a general rules is: *Don't be distracting.* But one thing does occur time and again which is, in fact, very distracting. When the speaker is finished using their visual aid, they leave it in the audience's view. Props are left on top of the lectern, slides remain visible until the next one gets discussed, and flipcharts are left on the last page, forgotten for the remainder of the presentation.

Leaving the prop in full view supplies a distraction. Members of your audience are so tempted to keep looking at what's in front of them, they cannot possibly give their undivided attention to the speaker.

Do yourself a favour. Remove as many distractions as possible, including your own visual aid.

## SHOW ITEMS ON A LIST ONE AT A TIME

Many people have caught on to the effectiveness of this technique and you will see it used almost everywhere. It is a good way to use a list while keeping your audience's attention. But just be sure you don't become a distraction yourself.

On overheads, for example, use a piece of paper to cover the lower portion of the list. As you move the paper, be careful not to shake it. Lay the paper down, and then let go of it so it doesn't shake.

When using a flipchart, write the list out on multiple pages, with the next page containing the same information as the previous page, plus one more item. Then flip the pages as you move down the list.

Using this technique is a good way to keep your audience's attention – and to keep a bit of suspense going as well.

## GIVE THEM TIME TO READ

Whenever you show a new slide, flipchart page or prop, you need to give the audience a few seconds to absorb the information. They need time to look at the pictures and read the words.

The problem arises when you don't allow them the time they need. You see, they'll just take the time anyway! But if you have continued on with your presentation, they may have missed some important information.

If you graciously allow them the time to read, they will be more than willing to give their attention back to you when you're ready to move on.

# 6 MAKE THEM REMEMBER YOU

"If we all did the things we are
capable of doing, we would
literally astound ourselves."

~ Thomas Edison

## INVOLVE YOUR AUDIENCE

One of the best ways to get your audience to remember you is to involve them somehow in our presentation. Audience involvement can range from a minor bit of participation to a full-blown team exercise.

Ask them questions and ask for a physical response (hands up, stand up, speak up). Have individual involvement (do exercises in a workbook, stand up and touch their toes).

Get them involved in a partner-type activity (ask a partner questions or shake hands with everyone around them). And of course, you can get them out of their seats and into a corner to participate in a team exercise.

Whatever method(s) you choose, be certain the exercise itself applies directly to the information or concepts you are discussing. That will help make the involvement meaningful and more than just a stretch break.

## HAVE SOMETHING UNUSUAL

When we see something unusual, we not only pay attention, but we are also more apt to retain the image longer. This is where you have some fun using your imagination, and very often, the wilder the better.

If you relate life to a bicycle ride, bring in the bicycle seat. Make an acronym out of your main points (i.e., A.E.R.O.) and bring a giant AERO chocolate bar. Better yet, give everyone their own AERO bar.

If you're discussing a foreign country, bring in an unusual artifact from that country. Something that has an unusual appearance, sound, or use will be remembered for a long time.

Sometimes an unusual visual aid can be used in a dramatic and certainly memorable grand entrance. Ride in on a horse, or walk in playing a set of bagpipes! Just be certain to have some assistance in removing the aid immediately after you have achieved the desired result.

## GIVE THEM SOMETHING

We all love to receive things and there are about as many ways to give people things as there are imaginations. Not only will they appreciate it at the time, but they'll remember it – and you – every time they come across your 'gift.'

The most common giveaways are handouts. Be imaginative. Use coloured paper and include a one-page summary sheet at the end. AERO bars for everyone (you can get miniature size) make a huge impact, and your audience is more likely to remember what the letters stand for.

Balloons, candy, door prizes, magic wands, and company memorabilia are also hits. Use your imagination and your budget creatively and you will leave a lasting impression.

## CREATE PICTURES IN THEIR MINDS

Pictures enhance retention. When people can visualize what you're saying and you can combine that with emotion of some kind, you will have them hooked. The trick is to be visually descriptive in your words and your actions.

Describe a scene in colourful yet simple words so your audience can *see* the scenery, *hear* the sounds, *smell* the aromas, *taste* the flavours, and *feel* the textures. Using the five senses to create pictures in people's minds is very effective.

Changing numbers and numerical data into pictures is imperative. Graphs and pie charts, grids, and lines all *show* what your mean. Words like 'half' and 'double' are easier to visualize than '50%' and '200%.'

## BE ENTHUSIASTIC

Ralph Waldo Emerson once said, "Nothing great was ever achieved without enthusiasm." If you want to be a powerful speaker, you must be enthusiastic. Hopefully you are passionate about your subject matter, so being enthusiastic should be easy!

But sometimes people are afraid to let their passion and emotion shine through. Very often the element of nervousness plays a big part in holding back emotions. But if you're going to be a powerful presenter, you must get past that and let it all hang out.

Letting your emotions show doesn't necessarily mean you have to be a sniffling, snuffling sop, but it does mean you have to get excited. Get mad! Be sympathetic! Be energetic! Remember Emerson's words and allow yourself to be GREAT!

# ABOUT THE AUTHOR

Dawn, husband John, and sons BJ, Brandon, Cameron and Dylan live in Caledon, Ontario, Canada.  Originally trained as a computer professional, Dawn first became interested in public speaking after joining a Toastmasters club.

After becoming involved in corporate training in 1992, Dawn found a new love as a corporate trainer teaching presentation skills.  Many workshops and seminars have been developed out of a passion for subjects she studied and those that made the biggest impact in her own professional advancement.  Basic and Advanced Presentation Skills and Leadership are a few of the areas in which Dawn excels both as a trainer and as a follower of the principles.

A love of learning and a deep desire to help others motivates Dawn as she continually learns new skills and shares what she learns with others.

As a dedicated mother, author, professional and Toastmaster, Dawn wants to help those she meets UNLEASH THEIR POTENTIAL!

Dawn Frail
25 Great Lakes Drive, Box 68600
Brampton, Ontario, Canada  L6R 0J8
519-927-1730
dawn@dawnfrail.com
www.dawnfrail.com